Learn Piano the Easy Way

USING SIMPLIFIED CHORDS

by
Paolo S. Ocampo

Learn Piano the Easy Way

1   Table of Contents

Table of Contents

Introduction

Learn Piano the Easy Way is a beautifully illustrated book designed to **teach** you how to **play** the **piano quickly** and **easily**.

Unlike traditional piano lessons that cover a lot of **complicated theory**, this book will show you the **secret shortcuts** to **playing popular hit songs** that you hear on the radio.

Did you know that you can play almost any song by memorizing only **12 Major Chords**?

A **Major Chord** is comprised of only **three notes** and are **super easy** to **remember. Chords** are how **pop bands** play their **music. Chords** are how **casual piano players** play and **sing along** with their family and friends. Learning how to play **chords** is the **easiest, fastest** and the **most fun way** to **play** the **piano**.

This book uses a **different approach** to **learning chords** - instead **memorizing** over a hundred different chords - you'll learn how to **derive** any chord from just **12 Chords**! This book will **teach** you how to use **simple formulas** to figure out how to **play any chord** for any song.

Included are many easy to follow **visual instructions** with **easy** to read **cheat sheets**. Also included are **resources** and **software** that you can use to **quickly learn**, **transcribe**, and **create music** to jam with - using **chords**!

In this book, you'll learn:

- How to make sense of the **piano keyboard**
- How to name all the **black** and **white keys** in the piano keyboard
- How to find the **notes that blend** with each black and white key
- How to easily find the **Major Chord** for **each key**
- How to play **Chord Variations** using **simple formulas** (no memorization!)
- The **simplified versions** of complicated **Chord Variations**
- How to add **piano grooves** using **Rhythm Patterns**
- How to figure out which **Chords** go **well together**
- How to hear **song patterns** using **Chord Progressions**
- Where to find **chords** and **lyrics** to jam with
- What **software** to use to **transcribe** the **chords** of any song
- Any many more!

Playing the piano is one of the simple joys in life. When you play the piano, time seems to stop. You'll enjoy many hours relaxing, playing and singing your favorite songs. I hope that you'll enjoy this book as much as I enjoyed writing it. Take the time and invest in learning this new skill. I promise that it will provide you with a lifetime of fun and relaxation.

The Piano Keyboard

Let's get to know your **piano keyboard**.

Black Keys/ White Keys

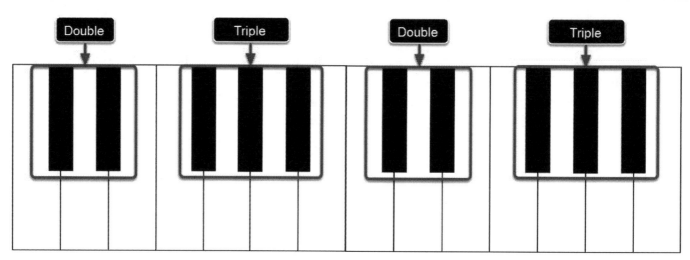

If you look at your keyboard, you will see that it has a **repeating set** of **2 Black Keys**, then **3 Black Keys**.

The Octave

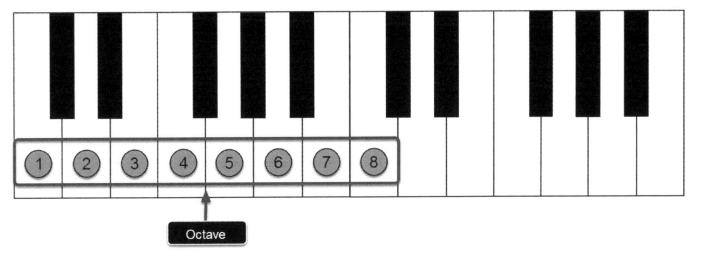

Octave

From the **white key on the left** of the **2 black keys**, to the **next white key on the left** of the **next 2 black keys**, is called on **Octave**. This is because the **distance** from the **first white key** to the **last white key** is exactly **8 white keys**.

You piano **keyboard** is actually just a **repeating set** of these **Octaves**.

The White Keys (Normal Keys)

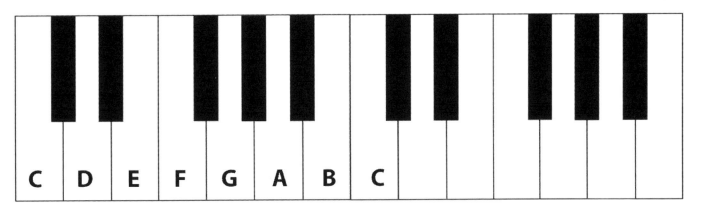

The white keys on each octave are called **C,D,E, F, G, A, B, C** respectively. These are called the **Normal Keys**.

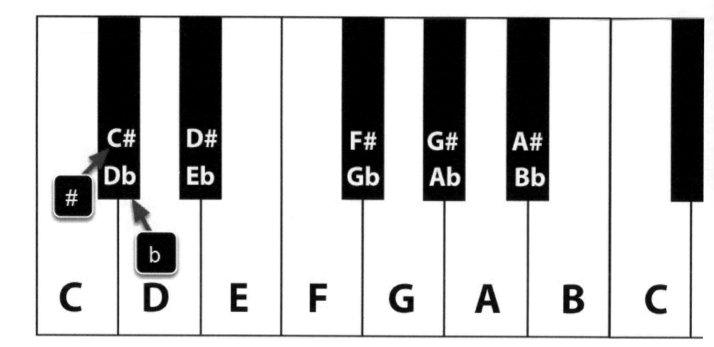

The names the **black keys** are based on the **white keys adjacent** to it.

- If the **black key** is on the **left**, it will be a **flat key** (indicated by a lowercase **b**)
- If the **black key** is on the **right**, it will be a **sharp key** (indicated by a hashtag **#**)

So this means that **every black key will have two names** - a **flat** (b) and a **sharp** (#). The names of the black keys are **interchangeable**.

Although you can switch between the two names of the black keys, more often than not, you will find that **C#**, **Eb**, **F#**, **Ab**, and **Bb** are used for naming the black keys.

Moving forward, we will be using these names for naming the black keys.

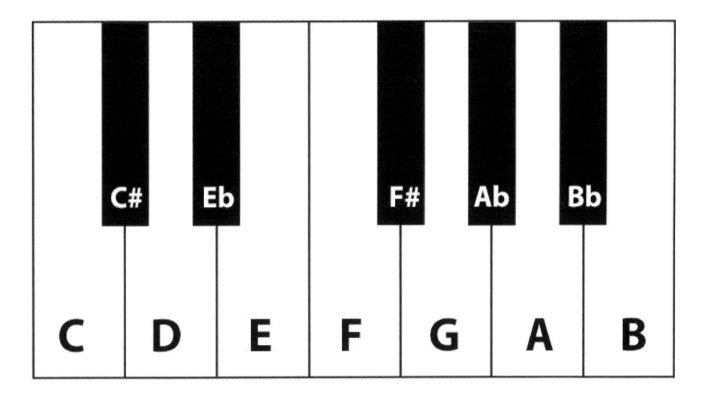

So, if we **combine the black and white keys**, there will be a **total of 12 keys - C**, **C#**, **D**, **Eb**, **E**, **F**, **F#**, **G**, **Ab**, **A**, **Bb** and **B**.

Download and print the **12 Keys Cheatsheet** :

http://webspicer.com/piano/12keys.pdf

Important:
You will need to **memorize** the names of these **12 keys** by heart, because this is the foundation of **playing piano chords**.

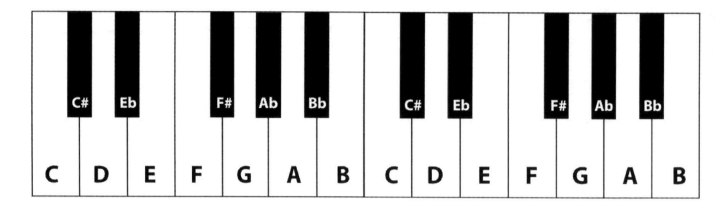

We already know that the keyboard is just a **repeating set of octaves**. Therefore, we can simply name all the keys in the piano the same way we named the keys in an octave.

Happy Birthday

Play the song by pressing the corresponding key

      F   C

Happy birthday to you

      C   F

Happy birthday to you

      C   Bb

Happy birthday dear Johnny

      F   G F

Happy birthday to you

The 12 Keys

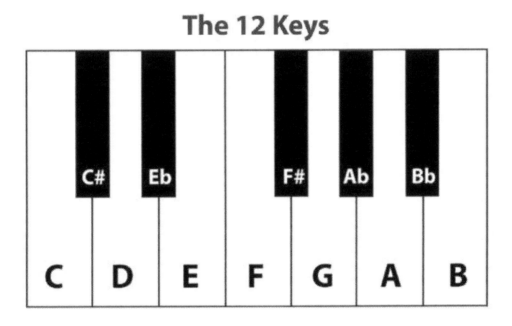

You can actually start playing basic piano by simply knowing the names of the **12 keys**.

In this example, press the apprporiate key indicated by the letter above the word as you sing the song. Notice how the key blends well with the melody.

Now try pressing the keys **on different octaves** and you will notice that even on different octaves, pressing the key of the same name will still **blend with the song**.

Download and Print: **Happy Birthday - Single Keys**

http://webspicer.com/piano/happy-birthday-1.pdf

The Major Scales

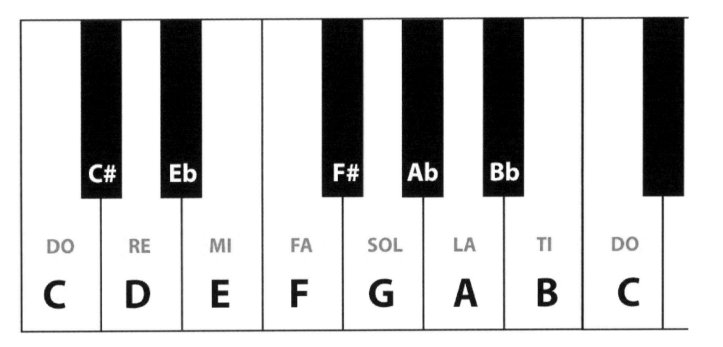

Major Scale = Do, Re, Mi …

The **Major Scale** is a set of **8 notes** that sound like **Do**, **Re**, **Mi**, **Fa**, **Sol**, **La**, **Ti**, **Do**.

For **every key** in the keyboard, there is a corresponding **Major Scale**.

Finding the Major scale is easy, because it always starts with the base key (Do), then just keep moving to the right until you hear (Re), then (Mi), and so on…

Below are the **Major Scales** for all the **12 keys**.

The C Major Scale

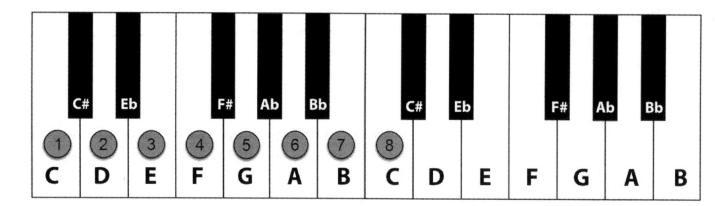

The C Major Scale - C, D, E, F, G, A, B, C

The C# Major Scale

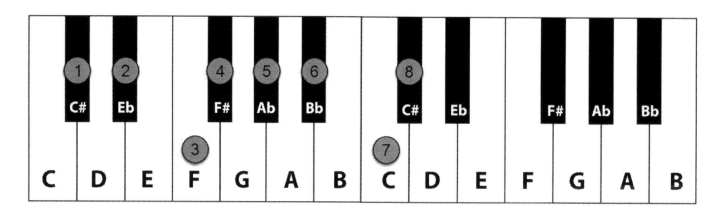

The C# Major Scale - C#, Eb, F, F#, Ab, Bb, C, C#

The D Major Scale

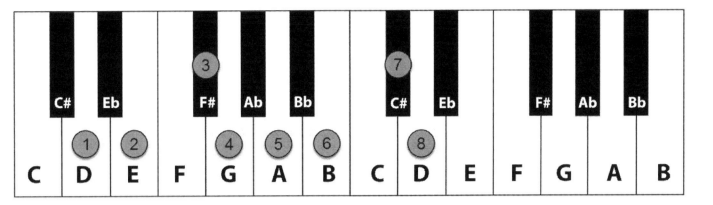

The D Major Scale - D, E, F#, G, A, B, C#, D

The Eb Major Scale

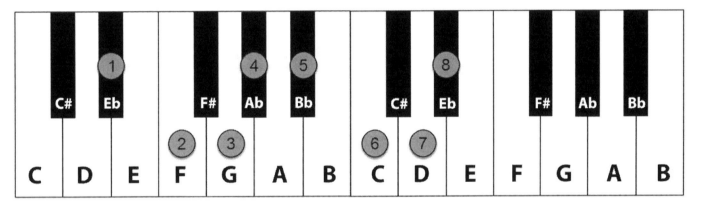

The Eb Major Scale - Eb, F, G, Ab, Bb, C, D, Eb

The E Major Scale

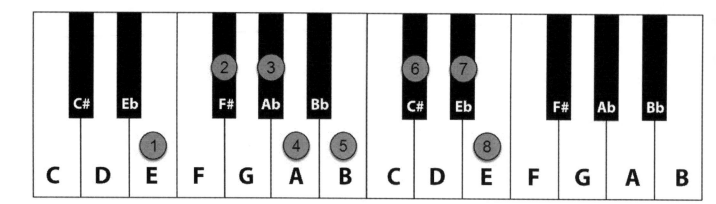

The E Major Scale - E, F#, Ab, A, B, C#, Eb, E

The F Major Scale

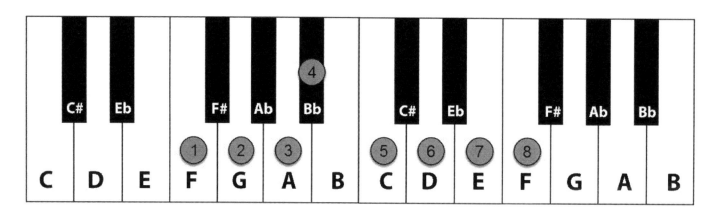

The F Major Scale - F, G, A, Bb, C, D, E, F

The F# Major Scale

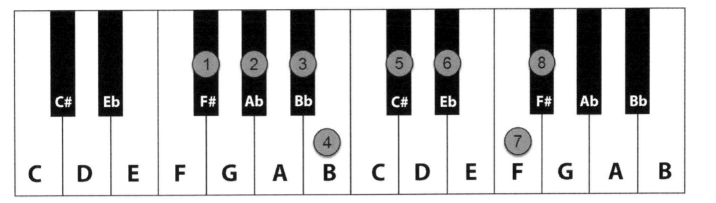

The F# Major Scale - F#, Ab, Bb, B, C#, Eb, F, F#

The G Major Scale

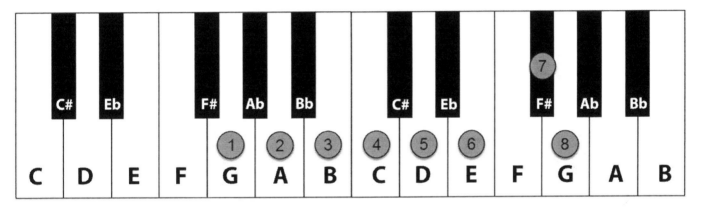

The G Major Scale - G, A, B, C, D, E, F#, G

The Ab Major Scale

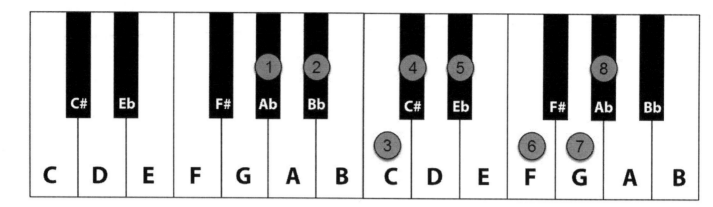

The Ab Major Scale - Ab, Bb, C, C#, Eb, F, G, Ab

The A Major Scale

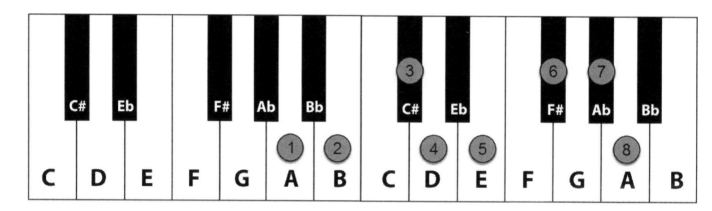

The A Major Scale - A, B, C#, D, E, F#, Ab, A

The Bb Major Scale

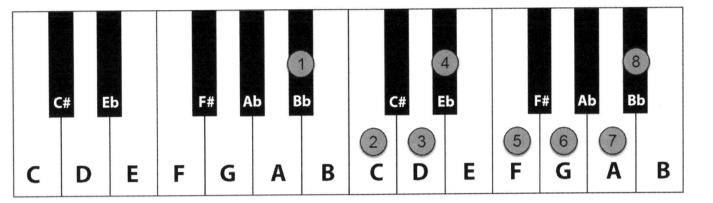

The Bb Major Scale - Bb, C, D, Eb, F, G, A, Bb

The B Major Scale

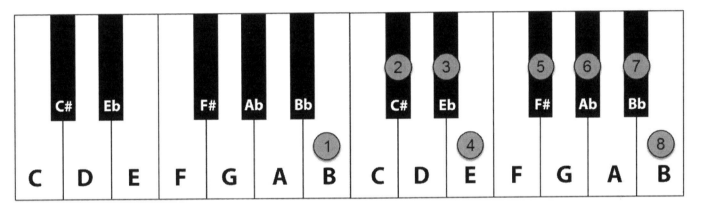

The B Major Scale - B, C#, Eb, E, F#, Ab, Bb, B

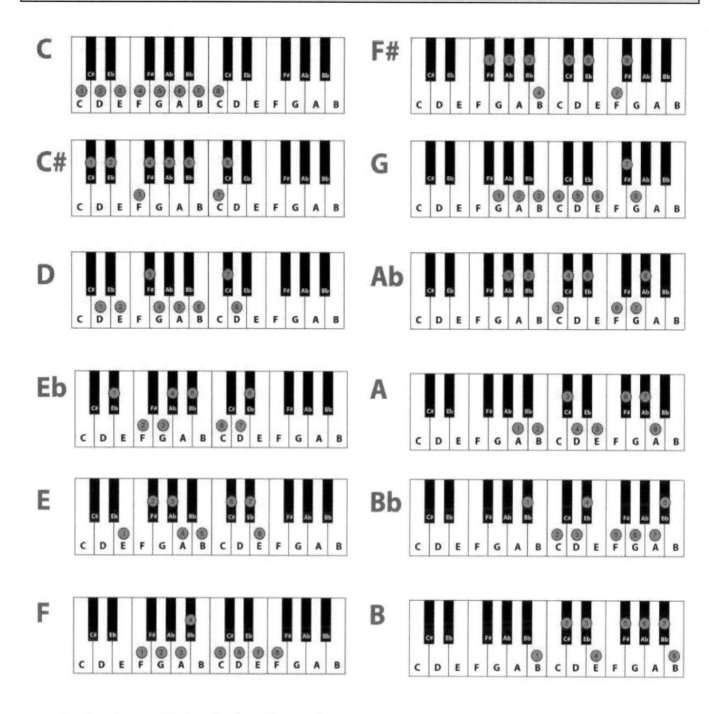

Download and Print: **Major Scales Cheat Sheet**

http://webspicer.com/piano/major-scales.pdf

Note:

If you are having a hard time memorizing the Major Scales, don't worry. Memorizing them is not required to play the piano. Right now, what's important is that you understand that the **Major Scales** sound like **Do, Re, Mi, Fa, Sol, La, Ti, Do**.

Playing the Major Chords

What are Chords?

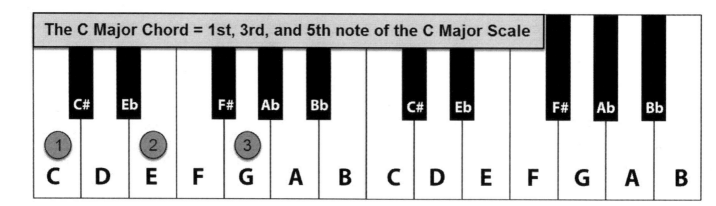

The C Major Chord = 1st, 3rd, and 5th note of the C Major Scale

A chord is a **set of notes** that **harmonize** with each other.

A **Major Chord** is the **1st**, **3rd**, and **5th** notes of the **Key's Major Scale**.

For example:

C Major Chord = 1st, 3rd, 5th of the C Major Scale = **C**, **E**, and **G**.
D Major Chord = 1st, 3rd, 5th of the D Major Scale = **D**, **F#**, and **A**.

Major Chords are also known as **Chord Triads** because they always contain **3 notes**.

Pressing them one at a time will sound like "**Do**", "**Mi**", and "**Sol**".

You can play a chord by pressing all 3 keys **at the same time**.

Below are **The 12 Major Chords**. Try to press all 3 keys **at the same time**.

The C Major Chord

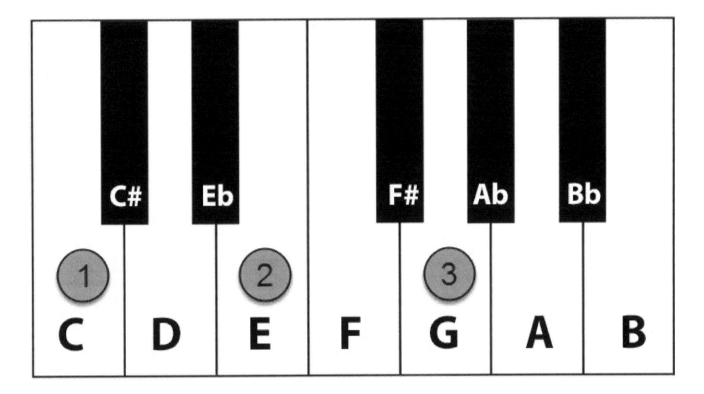

The C Major Chord - C, E, G

The C# Major Chord

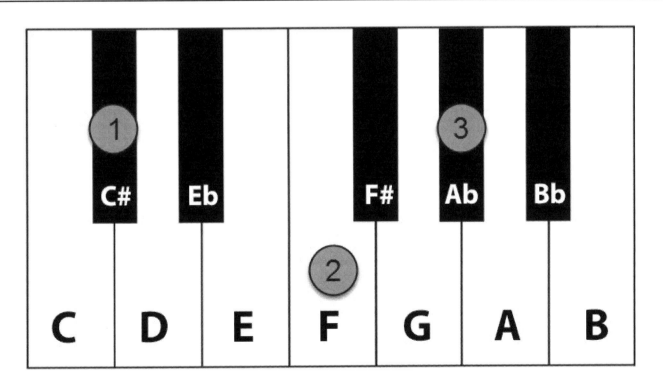

The C# Major Chord - C#, F, Ab

The D Major Chord

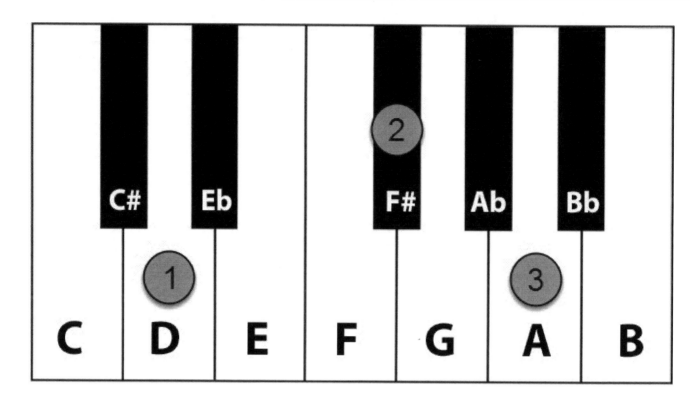

The D Major Chord - D, F#, A

The Eb Major Chord

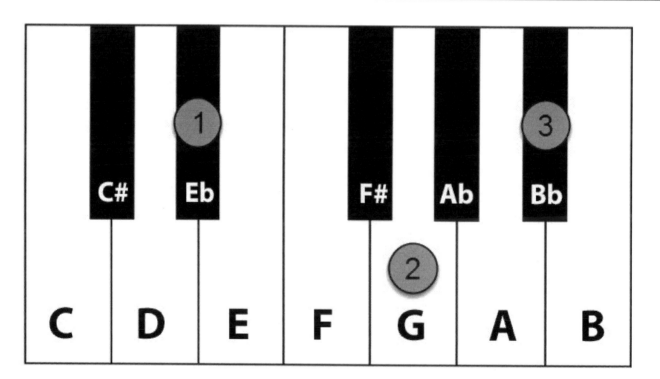

The Eb Major Chord - Eb, G, Bb

The E Major Chord

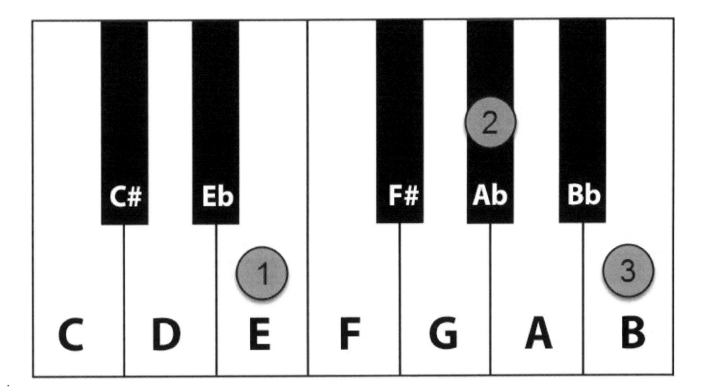

The E Major Chord - E, Ab, B

The F Major Chord

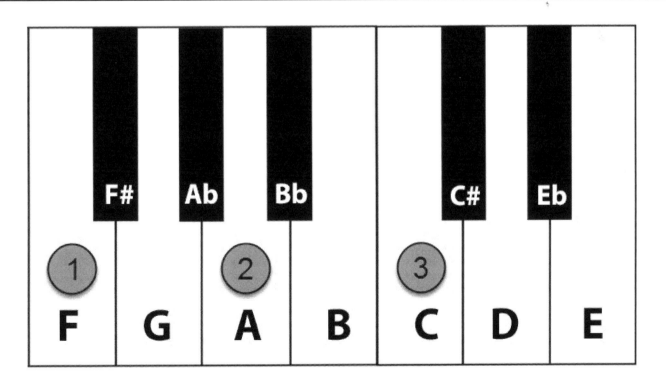

The F Major Chord - F, A, C

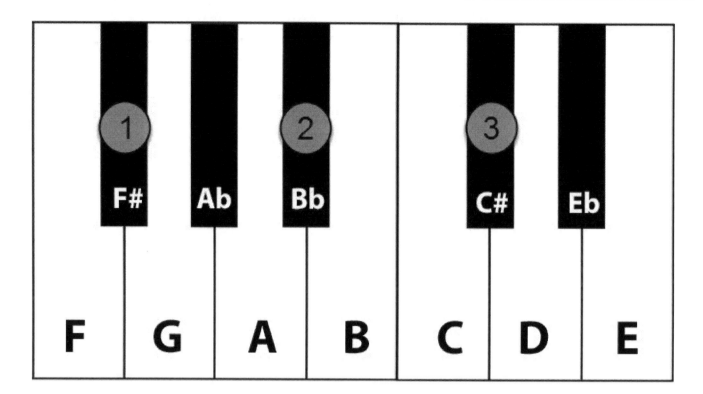

The F# Major Chord - F#, Bb, C#

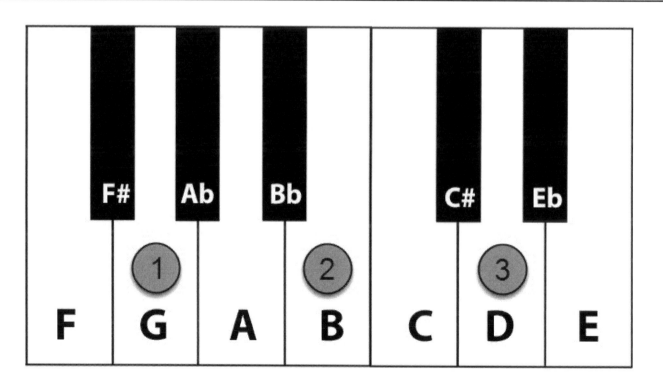

The G Major Chord - G, B, D

The Ab Major Chord

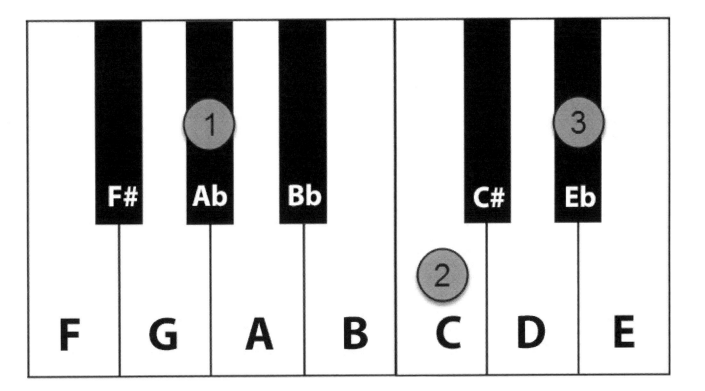

The Ab Major Chord - Ab, C, Eb

The A Major Chord

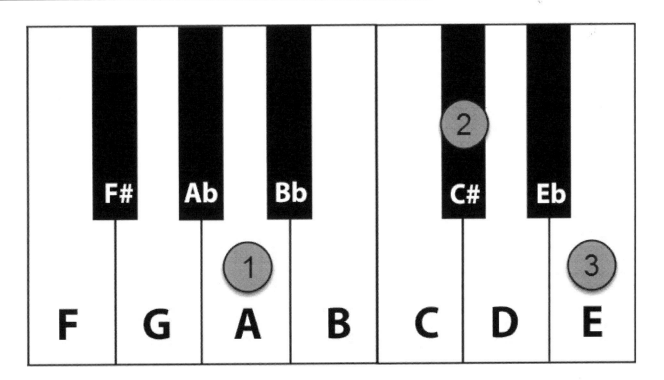

The A Major Chord - A, C#, E

The Bb Major Chord

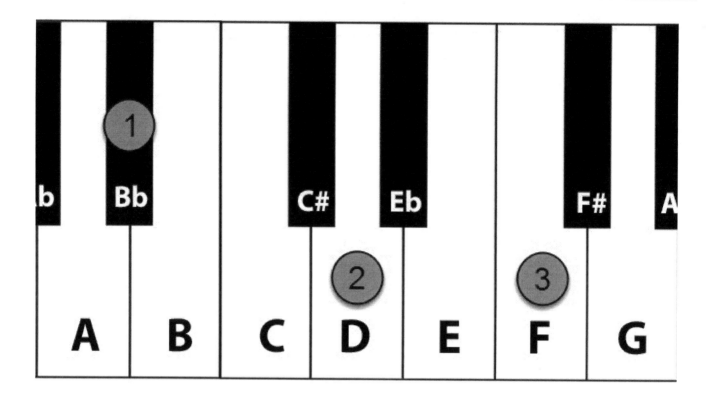

The Bb Major Chord - Bb, D, F

The B Major Chord

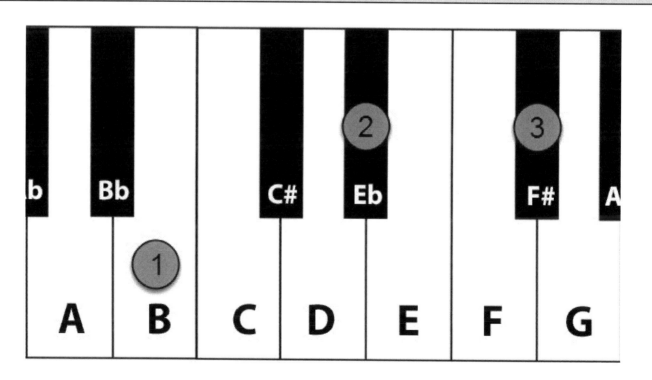

The B Major Chord - B, Eb, F#

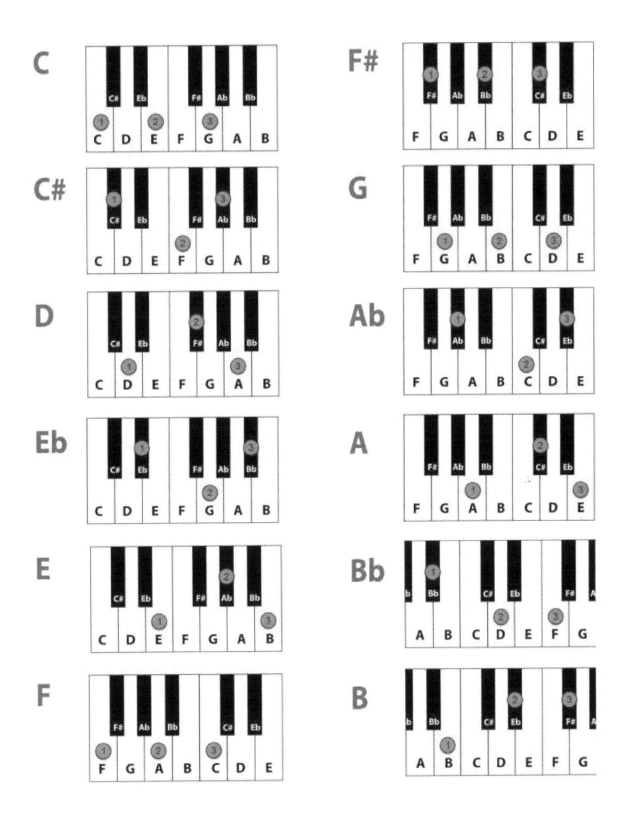

Download and Print: **Major Chords Cheat Sheet**

http://webspicer.com/piano/major-chords.pdf

Important:

Make sure to **memorize** the **12 Major Chords** - they are the **foundation** for the rest of the topics on this book.

If you are having a hard time memorizing the 12 Major Chords try this:

1. Start with the **Chord Key** (for example, the **C Major Chord** will start with the **C key**)
2. Start pressing keys on the right until they sound like - **Do**, **Re**, **Mi**, **Fa**, **Sol**
3. The **Major Chord** will be the keys that sound like **Do**, **Mi**, **Sol** (C, E and G)

Happy Birthday

Play the song by pressing the corresponding chord

     F   **C**

Happy birthday to you

     C   **F**

Happy birthday to you

     C   **Bb**

Happy birthday dear Johnny

     F   **G** **F**

Happy birthday to you

Chord Chart

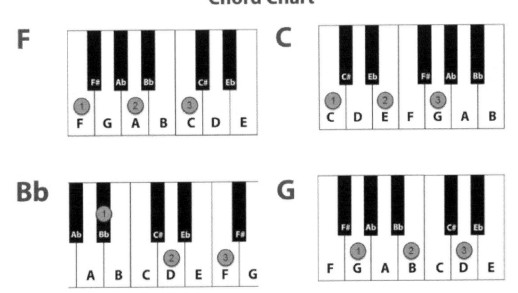

Now let's play the song Happy Birthday using **Major Chords**.

In this example, press the apprporiate **Major Chord** indicated by the **letter above the word** as you sing the song. Notice how the piano is now **blending** with the song with more **harmony**? Cool eh?

Now try pressing the keys **on different octaves** and you will notice that even on different octaves, pressing the key of the same name will still **blend with the song**.

Download and Print: **Happy Birthday - Major Chords**

http://webspicer.com/piano/happy-birthday-2.pdf

The Chord Variations

All songs can be played using the **12 Major Chords** as the foundation.

Although some songs can be played just using these **12 Major Chords**, most songs use these Major Chords **PLUS** its **Chord Variations**.

What are Chord Variations?

Chord Variations are **Major Chords** with **additional notes** to add **mood** to the chord.

A **chord variation** can make a **Major Chord** sound **gloomy**, **tense**, **cool**, **jazzy**, and so on.

There are **9 chord variations** for each **Major Chord** :

1.   Minor Chords
2.   Major 7th Chords
3.   7th Chords
4.   6th Chords
5.   9th Chords
6.   Augmented Chords
7.   Diminished Chords
8.   Suspended Chords
9.   Inverted Chords

Many aspiring piano players get **overwhelmed** with memorizing these **complex set of chord variations**. That's **12 Major Chords** times **9 Variations**! **108 Chords** to memorize! Yikes!!!

Not only that, many chord variations actually use **4 fingers** instead of just three. This requires an incredible amount of dexterity and many years of practice in order to master them.

Learn the Simpified Chord Variations:

Unless you will be playing piano professionally, pressing 3 notes instead of 4 notes won't really make a difference when you play a song. Using the simplified 3 finger chord variations will only require a few weeks of practice, instead of years.

In this chapter, you will learn how to **derive chord variations** based on the **12 Major Chords**.

There is no need to memorize all **108 chords**, just memorize the **12 Major Chords**, and the **9 formulas** of its **Chord Variations**.

With this knowledge, you can easily play along any song that you like

Actually, most pop and rock songs will only use the Major Chords, Minor Chords, 7th Chords, Suspended Chords, Slash Chords and Inverted Chords. So if you're just planning to jam with these types of music, you can survive by memorizing the formula of those five chord variations. The rest of the chord variations are usually used by Power Ballads, Jazz and R&B.

Below are the **formulas** for **deriving** the **chord variations**:

The C Major Chord

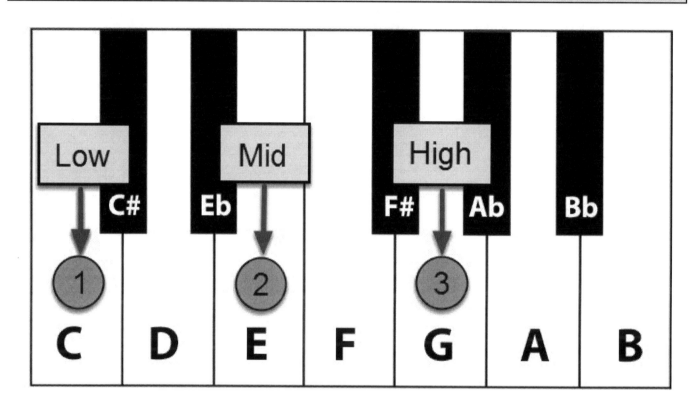

We know the each of the **12 Major Chords** contain exactly **3 notes**.

In the example above, the **C Major Chord** contains **C**, **E**, and **G**. Let's call them the following:

Left Note   = **Low**
Middle Note = **Mid**
Right Note   = **High**

We will now use this terminology to **derive** the **Chord Variations** for the **C Major Chord**.

Minor Chords (m)

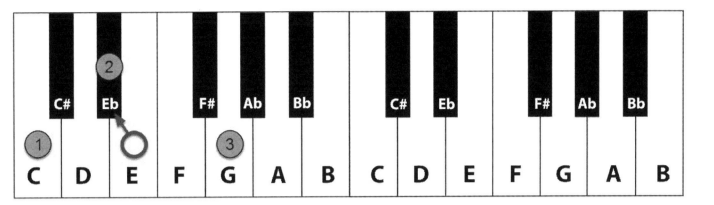

Minor Chords are suffixed with the small letter **m**.

Minor Chords add a hint of **sadness** to the **Major Chords**. These are commonly used by songs that sound sad.

Formula for Minor Chords = Mid - 1

For example, to derive the **Cm** (C minor) chord, move the **Middle Note one key to the left**.

So, **Cm** = **C, Eb, G**

Important:
You need to move notes **regardless** of the **Major Scale**. For example, **Eb** is on the left of **E**, but **Eb** is **not** on the **C Major Scale** (all white keys). So when moving notes, you'll need to move it on the **immediate left** or **right** of the note and **not based** on the **Key's Major Scale**.

Major 7 Chords (M7)

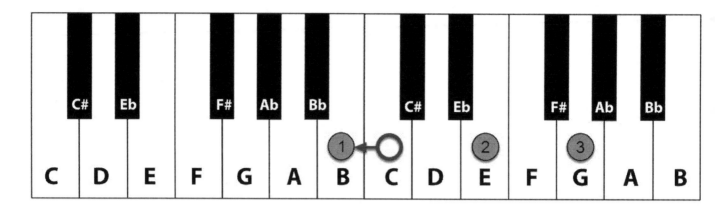

Major Seventh Chords are suffixed with the capital letter **M** and the number **7**.

Major Seventh Chords add a **cool** or **mellow** feel to the **Major Chord**.

Formula for Major Seventh Chords = Low - 1

For example, to derive the **CM7** (C Major Seventh) chord, move the **Low Note one key to the left**.

So, **CM7 = B, E, G**

7th Chords (7)

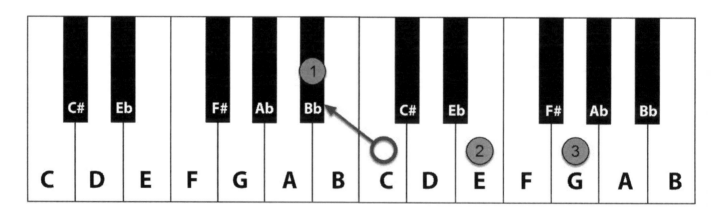

Seventh Chords are suffixed with the number **7**.

Seventh Chords add a hint of **tension** to the **Major Chord**.

Formula for Seventh Chords = Low - 2

For example, to derive the **C7** (C Seventh) chord, move the **Low Note two keys to the left**.

So, **C7** = **Bb, E, G**

6th Chords (6)

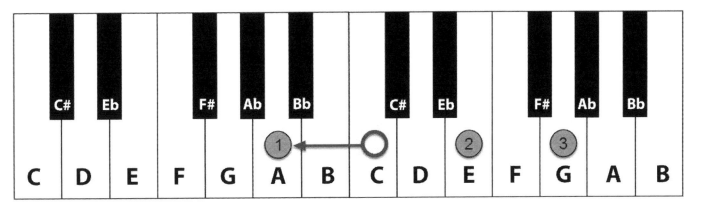

Sixth Chords are suffixed with the number **6**.

Sixth Chords add a **relaxing** or **calm** feeling to the **Major Chord**.

Formula for Sixth Chords = Low - 3

For example, to derive the **C6**(C Sixth) chord, move the **Low Note three keys to the left**.

So, **C6** = **A, E, G**

9th Chords (9)

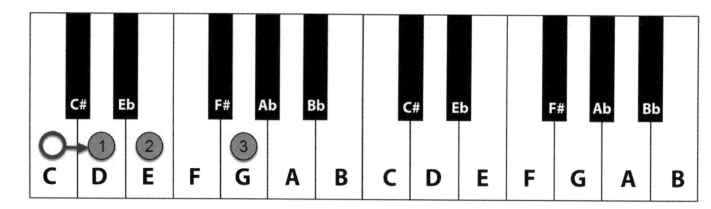

Ninth Chords are suffixed with the number **9**.

Ninth Chords add a feeling of **playfulness** to the **Major Chord**.

Formula for Ninth Chords = Low + 2

For example, to derive the **C9**(C Ninth) chord, move the **Low Note two keys to the right**.

So, **C9 = D, E, G**

Augmented Chords (aug)

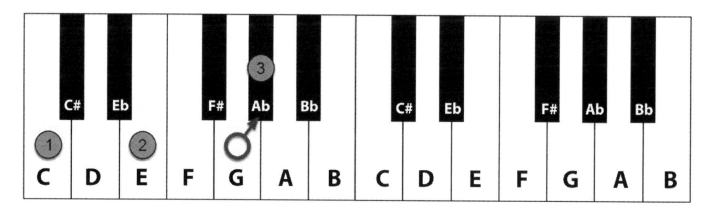

Augemented Chords are suffixed with word **aug**.

Augmented Chords add a feeling of **movement and suspense** to the **Major Chord**.

Formula for Augmented Chords = High + 1

For example, to derive the **Caug**(C Augmented) chord, move the **High Note one key to the**

right.

So, **Caug** = **C, E, Ab**

Diminished Chords (dim)

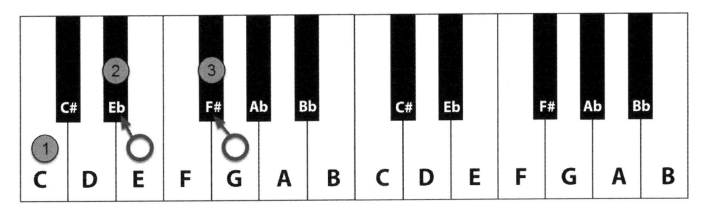

Diminished Chords are suffixed with word **dim**.

Diminished Chords add a **dark and edgy** feeling to the **Major Chord**.

Formula for Diminished Chords = Mid - 1, High - 1

For example, to derive the **Cdim**(C Diminished) chord, move the **Middle and High Notes one key to the left**.

So, **Cdim** = **C, Eb, F#**

Suspended Chords (sus)

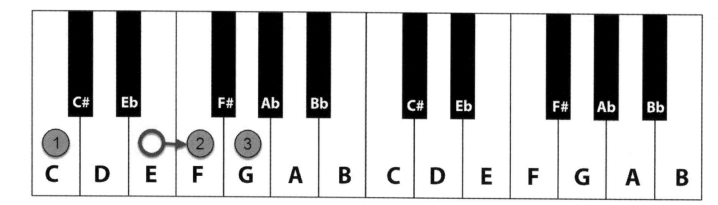

Suspended Chords are suffixed with word **sus**.

Suspended Chords add a feeling of **suspension** and is often **followed** by the **Base Chord**.

Formula for Suspended Chords = Mid + 1

For example, to derive the **Csus**(C Suspended) chord, move the **Middle Note one key to the right**.

So, **Csus = C, F, G**

Inverted Chords

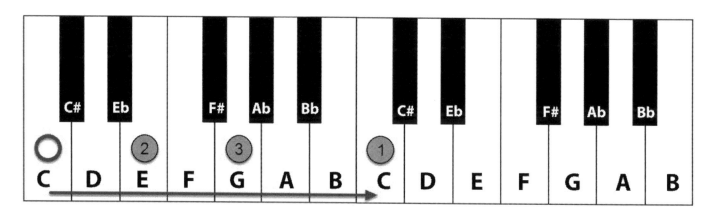

Inverted Chords are **Major Chords** pressed in a **different sequence**.

Inverted Chords are not written differently than Major Chords, but sometimes you use it to make it **easier** to **change from one chord to another**.

Formula for Inverted Chords = Press the Low and/or Middle Note one octave higher

For example, to derive the **Inverted C Major Chord**, move the **Low Note one octave higher**

So, **C** = **E, G, C**

Or, you can also move the **Low and Middle Notes one octave higher:**

C = **G, C, E**

As long as you are pressing **C**, **E**, or **G** regardless of the sequence, you are pressing the **C Major Chord**.

Combining Chord Variations

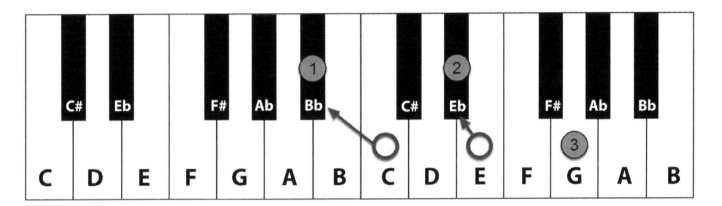

You can also **combine** Chord Variations.

For example, you can use the **Cm7** (C Minor 7th) chord which is a combination of a **Minor Chord** and a **7th Chord**.

We know that:

Minor Chord (m) = **Mid -1**
Seventh Chord (7) = **Low - 2**

For example, to derive the **Cm7**(C Minor 7th) chord, move the **Middle Note one key to the left, and Low Note two keys to the left**.

So, **Cm7** = **Bb, Eb, G**

The Simplified Chord Chart Cheat Sheet

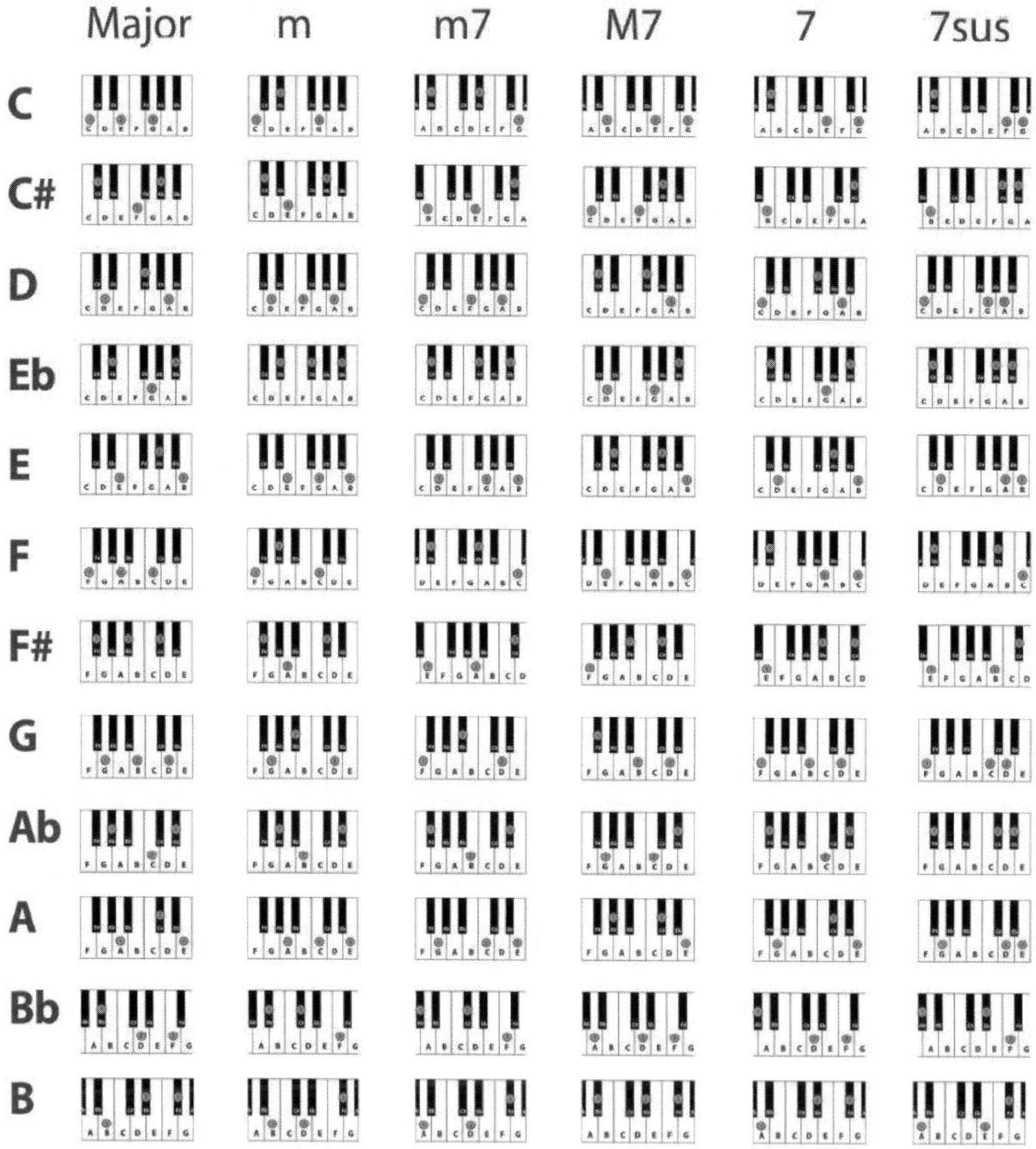

	sus	9	9sus	6	aug (+)	dim(°)
C						
C#						
D						
Eb						
E						
F						
F#						
G						
Ab						
A						
Bb						
B						

Download and Print: **The Simplified Chord Chart**

http://webspicer.com/piano/chord-chart-1.pdf
http://webspicer.com/piano/chord-chart-2.pdf

Using this Cheat Sheet, you can play any song that you can think of.
Even better, just memorize the **12 Major Chords** from the previous chapter, and use the **Chord Variation Formulas** you learned in this chapter to derive the chord that you need.

The Chord Variation Formulas Cheat Sheet

Chord Variation Formulas

Based on the 3 Notes of the Major Chord

Chord Name	Symbol	Formula
Minor	m	Mid - 1
Major Seventh	M7	Low - 1
Seventh	7	Low - 2
Sixth	6	Low - 3
Ninth	9	Low + 2
Augmented	aug or +	High + 1
Diminished	dim or °	Mid - 1, High - 1
Suspended	sus	Mid + 1

Download and Print: **Chord Variation Formulas Cheat Sheet**

http://webspicer.com/piano/chord-formulas.pdf

Away in Manger

Play the song by pressing the corresponding chord
Derive the chord variation using the Chord Variation Cheat Sheet

    G   **G**   **C**   **G**
Away in a manger, no crib for a bed

D7   **D7**   **C**   **G**
The little Lord Jesus, laid down his sweet head

    G   **G**   **C**   **G**
The stars in the sky, looked down where He lay

    D7   **G**   **Am**   **G**
The little Lord Jesus, alseep on the hay

Major Chords

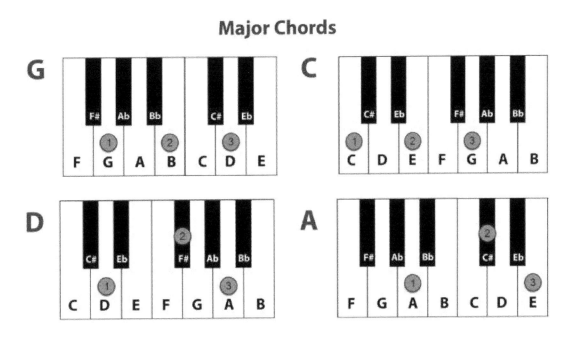

Now let's play the song "Away in a Manger" using **Major Chords** and **Chord Variations**.

In this example, press the appropriate **Major Chord** indicated by the **letter above the word.**

For the **chord variations**:

- **D7** – D Major Chord -> **Low - 2**
- **Am** = A Major Chord -> **Mid -1**

Download and Print: **Away in a Manger**

http://webspicer.com/piano/away-in-a-manger.pdf

Rhythm Patterns

What should I play on my left hand?

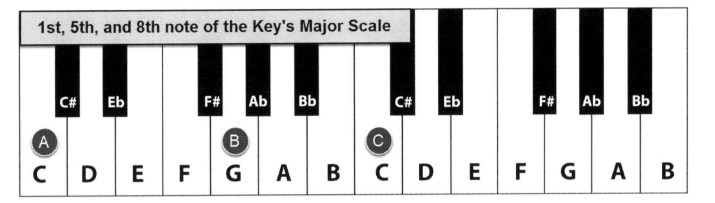

Playing chords is always done using the **right hand**. To create a **fuller sound**, you can also start playing keys using your **left hand**.

Playing with your **left hand** adds a **bass sound** to your chords.

So what keys should you play with your left hand? You have four options:

1. The **1st Note**
2. The **1st Note** and the **5th note**
3. The **1st Note** and the **8th note** (1st Note One Octave Higher)
4. The **1st**, **5th**, and **8th** notes of the **Key's Major Scale**

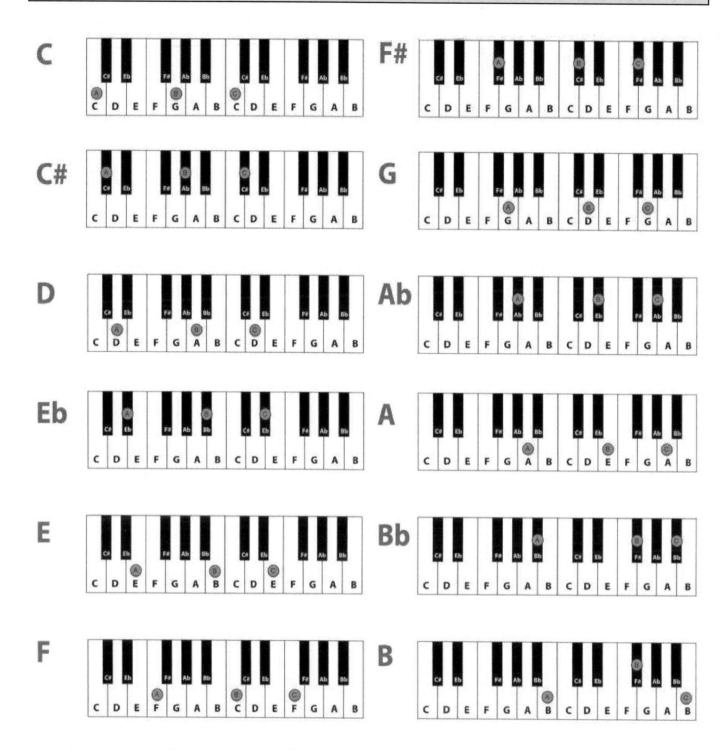

Download and Print: **The Left Hand Cheat Sheet**

http://webspicer.com/piano/left-hand.pdf

Important:

Whether playing a **Chord Variation** or a **Major Chord**, you will still press the **same keys** on the **left hand**.

So, if you are playing C, C9, C7, etc., you will still be pressing C, G, and C on your left hand (1st, 5th, and 8th notes of the Key's Major Scale).

What are Rhythm Patterns

Rhythm Patterns create a **rhythmic groove** when playing piano chords. The effect is is similar to **strumming a guitar**.

You can **change the mood** of a song simply by **changing the rhythmic pattern**.

You can play different rhythm patterns by changing the timing of the left and right hands.

Below are some easy rhythm patterns to get you started.

The Pulse

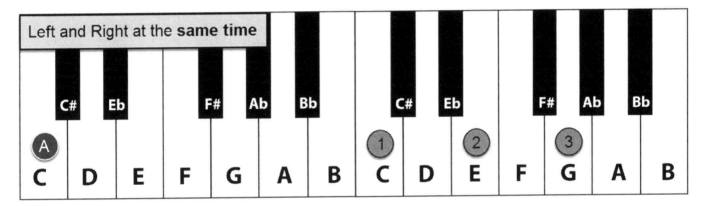

The **Pulse** is done by pressing the **left** and **right** hands **at the same time**.

This creates a **pulse sounding** ryhthm which is perfect if you are just learning to play a new song.

The Rocker

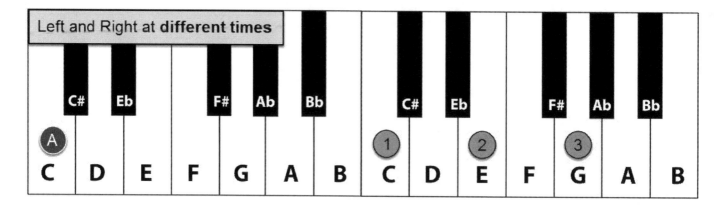

The Rocker is done by pressing the **left** and **right** hands **at the different times**.

This creates a **rocking motion** when you press the piano chords.

You can **mix and match** the left and right hands to create **different sounding rythms**. For example, you can do left (1x), right (5x) or do left(3x), right(3x) and so on.

The Arpeggio (Right Hand)

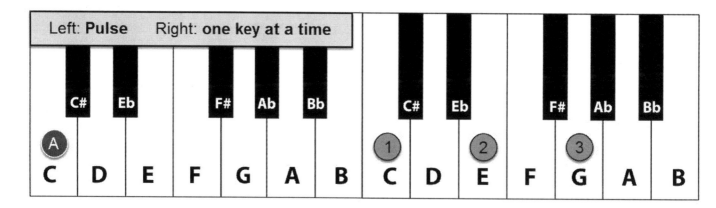

The Arpeggio (pronounced Arpe-Jee-Oh) means playing the **chords notes one at a time**, instead of all together.

This creates a **flowing rhythm** which is perfect for slower songs. You can do Arpeggios on the right hand, the left hand, or both

The Arpeggio (Left Hand)

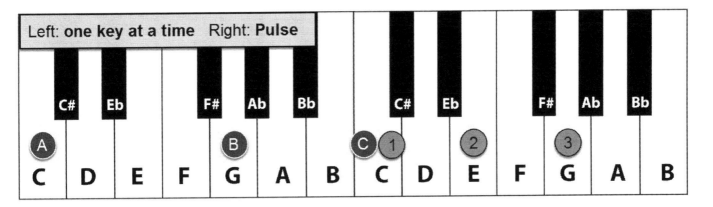

Here we see how to play Arpeggios on the **left hand**. You usually do left hand Arpeggios on the **1st**, **5th**, and **8th** notes.

The Arpeggio (Left Hand Multiple Octaves)

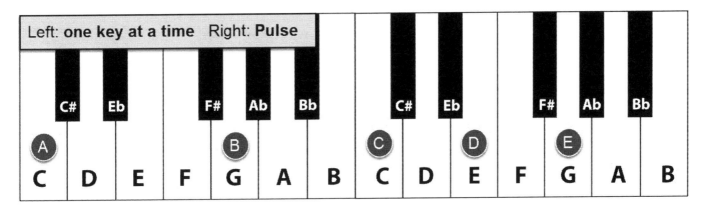

You can also span **multiple octaves** when playing Arpeggios on the left hand.

Just press the same **1st**, **5th**, and **8th** notes **on the first octave**, then the **Chord Notes** on the **next octave**. The **right hand** presses the **chord notes** on the **octave farther on the right**.

The Apreggio (Both Hands)

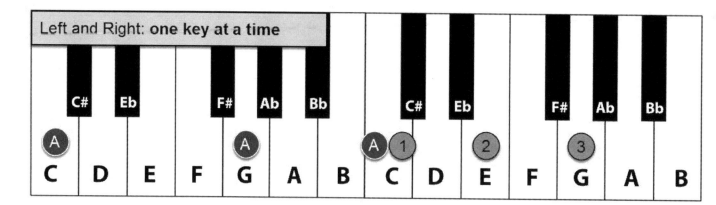

Now it's time to get jazzy! You can do **Arpeggios** on the **left** and **right hands**, and even **mix and match** it with **pulse** and **rocker** ryhthms!

It does not even matter **when you press the keys** as long as you press the **1st, 5th**, and **8th** keys on the **left**, and the **chord keys** on the **right**.

As long as you press the correct keys, you can play the song at your own rhythm.

Slash Chords

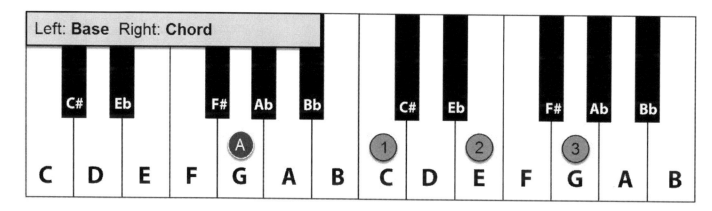

Slash Chords are **chords** that use a **different base** (left hand).

The **Base** is usually the **5th** or **4th** note on the **Key's Major Scale**. So on the **C chord**, you can have the **slash chords C/F** or **C/G**.

How to play Slash Chords:

C/G (C over G) means the right hand plays the **C chord**, but the left hand plays a **G key (Base)**.

Chord Progressions

What are Chord Progessions?

We already know that we only have **12 chords** to play around with - **C**, **C#**, **D**, **Eb**, **E**, **F**, **F#**, **G**, **Ab**, **A**, **Bb**, **B**.

Although we can mix and match all 12 chords to compose a song, most songwriters **do not randomly** use these **12 chords**. They follow a logical flow called a **Chord Progression**.

A **Chord Progession** is a **formula** for getting which **chords sound well** with other chords.

Learning about Chord Progessions is the first step to learning **how to play songs by ear**.

The Four Chord Special

The Four Chord Special
C, G, Am, F

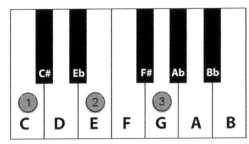
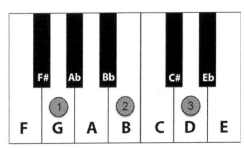
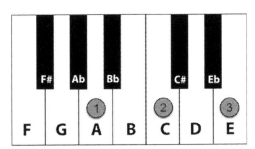
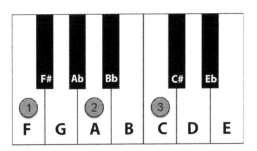

Here's a special treat for you. Did you know that you can play **most pop songs** using only **four chords**?

Yes, you can play many pop songs using these four chords **C**, **G**, **Am**, and **F chords** (super easy because they all use white keys).

The four chord special is popularized by the Youtubers **Axis of Awesome** and **Riptard**.

- webspicer.com/piano/4chords1
- webspicer.com/piano/4chords2

The **Chord Progession** used by these chords is called the **I–V–vi–IV** progression.

In this chapter, you will learn how to get this progression in **different keys** through **transposition**. You'll also learn the **most popular chord progressions** used by songwriters today.

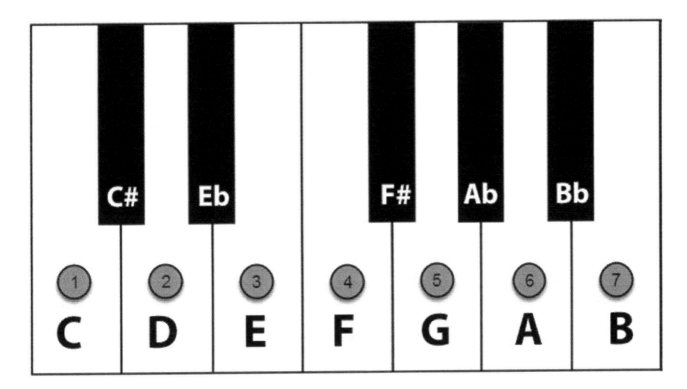

In the C Major Scale:

I	= 1st note	= C
V	= 5th note	= G
vi	= 6th note (minor)	= Am
IV	= 4th note	= F

Chord Progressions use a **Roman Numeral Chord Notation:**

Capital Roman Numerals = Major Chord
Small Roman Numerals = Minor Chord

The **Roman Number** corresponds to the **number of the note** in the **Key's Major Scale**.

For example, to get the **I-V-vi-IV** on the **C Major Scale**, we need to get the **1st, 5th, 6th,** and **4th** note (**C, G, A, F**).

But because the 6th (A) is a **small Roman Number** (vi), we need to make it a **Minor Chord** (Am).

So the **I-V-vi-IV** progression of the **C Major Scale** is - C, G, Am, F.

Note:

Chord Progressions are normally played In a normal seqeunce. But they can also be played in a different sequence - for exampe **vi-IV-I-V** (Am, F, C, G).

Transposing Chords

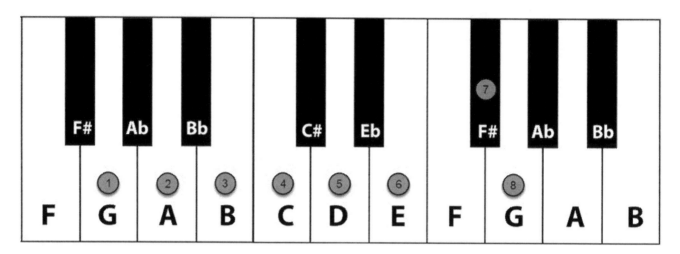

In the G Major Scale:

I	= 1st note	= G
V	= 5th note	= D
vi	= 6th note (minor)	= Em
IV	= 4th note	= C

Some singers can sing **high notes**, and some singers can sing **low notes**.

If you are having a hard time singing songs in the **C Major Scale**, you can **tranpose** the song to **fit your vocal range**.

For example, let's transpose the **I-V-vi-IV** progression in the **key of G**.

To **Tranpose Chords:**

1. Get the **Major Scale of the key** (G Major Scale).
2. Then simply follow the same formula - **I-V-vi-IV** = **G, D, Em, C**

Key	I	V	vi	IV
C	C	G	Am	F
C#	C#	Ab	Bbm	F#
D	D	A	Bm	G
Eb	Eb	Bb	Cm	Ab
E	E	B	C#m	A
F	F	C	Dm	Bb
F#	F#	C#	Ebm	B
G	G	D	Em	C
Ab	Ab	Eb	Fm	C#
A	A	E	F#m	D
Bb	Bb	F	Gm	Eb
B	B	F#	Abm	E

Download and Print: **The 4 Chord Special in all 12 Keys**

http://webspicer.com/piano/four-chords.pdf

Now try to sing the following songs on different keys to find your vocal range.

http://webspicer.com/piano/four-chord-songs.pdf

Note:
You can also use this online tool to transpose chords - http://tabtuner.com/.

The Circle of Fifths

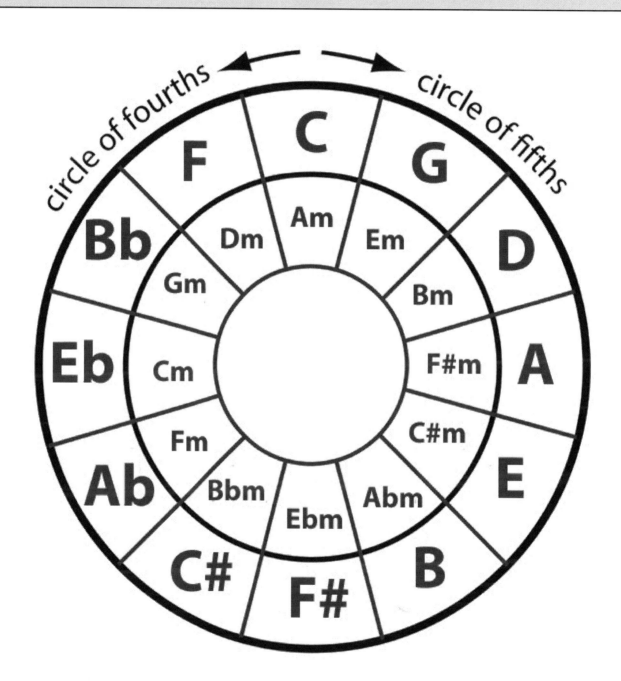

The **Circle of Fifths** is a handy tool for finding chords that go well with other chords.

It is also known as the **Circle of Fourths**, or the **Circle of Keys**.

Basically, you pick any chord in the circle, and the **chords adjacent** to it will **harmonize** well with that chord.

For example, if we pick:

- **C** - then **F** and **G** chords will harmonize wth it
- **Bb** - then **Eb** and **F** chords will harmonize with it
- **D** - then **A** and **G** chords will harmonize with it.

This is because for any given key, the **V** and **IV** notes in its **Major Scale** blends really well with the Base Key.

And if you look at the circle, you'll find that the key on the **right** of the key is the **5th note** of the key's major scale. And on the **left** is the **4th note** of the key's major scale.

Note:
So in any given chord progression, the **4th** and **5th** chords are the **most likely** to appear together with the Base Chord.

Download and Print: **The Circle of Fifths**

http://www.webspicer.com/piano/circle-of-fifths.pdf

Finding Minor Chords in the Circle

You can also find **Minor Chords** in the **Circle of Fifths**.

Minor Chords that will blend well with the Base Chord can be found at the **Inner Circle of the Circle of Fifths**. It will be the three Minor Chords **adjacent** to the Base Chord.

For example, if we pick:

- **C** - we get **Dm**, **Am** and **Em**
- **Bb** - we get **Cm**, **Gm** and **Dm**
- **D** - we get **Em**, **Bm** and **F#m**

The reason these minor chords blend well with the base key is because they are the **2nd**, **3rd**, **6th** chords on that key's **Major Scale**.

Note:

So after the **4th** and **5th** chords, the **most likely** chords to appear in a chord progression are the **2nd**, **3rd** and **6th Minor Chords**.

The **7th chord** is very rarely used in a Chord Progression.

Why use Minor Chords?

I - ii - iii - IV - V- vi - VIIdim

The Chords of the Major Scale

The reason that we are using **minor keys** is that in order to **harmonize** a key, **all the notes** used in a chord should come from the key's **Major Scale**.

For example, the **C Major Scale** has **all white keys**.

We can press the **C**, **F**, and **G** chords (**1st**, **4th** and **5th chords**) using **all white keys**.

However we cannot create the **D**, **E**, and **A** chords (**2nd**, **3rd** and **6th chords**) because they require **black keys**.

But if we change these chords to Minor Chords like **Dm**, **Em** and **Am,** then they will be using all white keys.

What about the 7th note?

The **7th note** is very rarely used in a chord progression. But if it comes up, it will be in the form of a **Diminished Chord**.

In the **Key of C**, the **7th note** is a **B**. Remember that all notes of a Chord should come from the Key's Major Scale (The C Major Scale has all White Keys).

The **B Chord** (B, Eb, F#) contains two Black Keys - Eb and F# . By making it a Diminished Chord (Mid - 1, High - 1), we can make it use all white keys. So, Bdim = B, E, and F (all white keys).

So in short, the harmonizing chords for any given key is this:

I - ii - iii - IV - V - vi - VIIdim

Note:

Notice that the **2nd**, **3rd** and **6th chords** are **minor chords**, and the **7th** is a **diminished** chord.

Key	I	ii	iii	IV	V	vi	VIIdim
C	C	Dm	Em	F	G	Am	Bdim
C#	C#	Ebm	Fm	F#	Ab	Bbm	Cdim
D	D	Em	F#m	G	A	Bm	C#dim
Eb	Eb	Fm	Gm	Ab	Bb	Cm	Ddim
E	E	F#m	Abm	A	B	C#m	Ebdim
F	F	Gm	Am	Bb	C	Dm	Edim
F#	F#	Abm	Bbm	B	C#	Ebm	Fdim
G	G	Am	Bm	C	D	Em	F#dim
Ab	Ab	Bbm	Cm	C#	Eb	Fm	Gdim
A	A	Bm	C#m	D	E	F#m	Abdim
Bb	Bb	Cm	Dm	Eb	F	Gm	Adim
B	B	C#m	Ebm	E	F#	Abm	Bbdim

Download and Print: **The Chords of the Major Scale**

http://webspicer.com/piano/major-scale-chords.pdf

The Most Popular Chord Progressions are created by mixing and matching these chords.

Complicated by Avril Lavigne ☆

Sections: ● Verse, ■ Pre-Chorus, ●● Chorus.
Contributors: mathiascg and socsy Plus. Learn how to contribute.
Genres: Alternative, Pop, Soul [Add/Edit ▾]

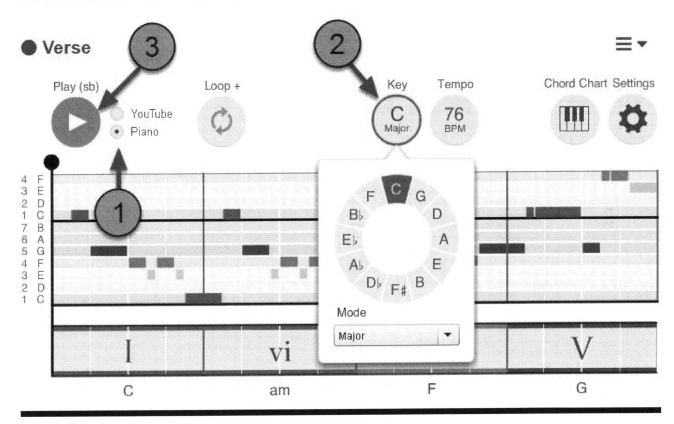

Now that you understand how to use the **Circle of Fifths**, and how **Chord Progressions** are derived, you can try out these **7 popular chord progressions**:

Note:
Remember that chords progressions are **usually played in sequence**, but sometimes the chords used by the progression can **mixed and matched** throughout the song.

The following songs use the Chord Progression in either their Verses, or Chorus.

Instruction: To hear the songs, go to : https://www.hooktheory.com/theorytab and search by song name. Then select **Piano** on the **Radio Button**, the **Key of C** on the **Circle of Fifths**, then **click Play**.

1. I - V - vi - IV (C, G, Am, F)

- Time After Time - Cindi Lauper

- Complicated - Avril Lavigne
- Grenade - Bruno Mars
- Jar of Hearts - Christina Perri
- 21 Guns - Green Day
- Im'Yours - Jason Mraz
- Paparazzi - Lady Gaga
- She will be loved - Maroon 5
- Let her go - Passenger
- I knew your were trouble - Taylor Swift

2. I-IV-V (C, F, G)

- Good Riddance - Green Day
- Sugar Sugar - The Archies
- Here Comes the Sun - Beatles
- Once Upon a Time in Your Wildest Dreams - The Moody Blues
- Leaving on a Jetplane - John Denver

3. I - vi - ii - V (C, Am, Dm, G)

- Last Christmas - Wham
- Over the Rainbow - Judy Garland
- This Love - Maroon 5
- Uptown Girl - Billy Joel
- I will - The Beatles

4. I - V - vi - iii (C, G, Am, Em)

- Canon in D Major - Johann Pachelbel
- Cryin - Aerosmith
- Basketcase - Green Day
- Firework - Katy Perry
- Under the Bridge - Red Hot Chili Peppers

5. Vi - V - IV - V (Am, G, F, G)

- Rolling in the Deep - Adele
- Just Can't get enough - Black Eyed Peas
- My heart will go on - Celine Dion

6. I - vi - IV - V (C, Am, F, G)

- I saw the sign - Ace of Base
- Girl on Fire - Alicia Keys
- Complicated - Avril Lavigne
- Stand by Me - Ben E. King
- Hallelujah - Jeff Buckley
- Baby - Justin Bieber
- Unwell - Matchbox 20
- Unchained Melody - Righteous Brothers
- Beautiful Girls - Sean Kingston
- Eternal Flame - The Bangles

7. I-IV (C,F)

- I love it - Icona Pop
- I melt with you - Modern English
- Mama Mia - Abba
- Total Eclipse of the Heart - Bonnie Tyler
- Everybody Hurts - REM

Need more chord progressions? Go here :
https://www.hooktheory.com/theorytab/common-chord-progressions

Play the songs based on your skill level: https://www.hooktheory.com/theorytab/difficulties

The 12 Bar Blues

C	C	C	C
F	F	C	C
G	F	C	C

There is another kind of progression called **The 12 Bar Blues**. It's an elongated variation of the **I - IV - V** Chord Progression.

You play blues like this:

I - Four Counts
IV - Two Counts
I - Two Counts
V - One Count
IV - One Count
I - Two Counts

Songs Using the 12 Bar Blues

Instruction: To hear the songs, go to : https://www.hooktheory.com/theorytab and search by song name. Then select **Piano** on the **Radio Button**, the **Key of C** on the **Circle of Fifths**, then **click Play**.

- Rock Around The Clock - Bill Haley and the Comets
- Tutti Frutti - Little Richard
- Johnny B. Goode - Chuck Berry
- Hound Dog - Elvis Presley
- Shake rattle and Roll - Joe Turner
- Give Me One Reason - Tracy Chapman

Software and Resources

You can find a lot of **websites** that will give you the **Chords** and **Lyrics** of many popular songs.

Here are the **Top 6** chord and lyrics websites:

1.   E-Chords - www.e-chords.com
2.   Chordie - www.chordie.com
3.   Ultimate Guitar - www.ultimate-guitar.com
4.   AZ Chords - www.azchords.com
5.   911 Tabs - www.911tabs.com
6.   Guitar Tabs - www.guitartabs.cc

Note:

Sometimes the **chords** on these websites are **not 100% accurate**. If you feel that the chord doesn't sound right, use the **Circle of Fifths** to find out which chords will blend with the song chords.

And here's a couple of lesser known Chords and Lyrics sites:

•   Classic Country Lyrics - www.classic-country-song-lyrics.com
•   PJ's Guitar Chords - www.guitarsongs.info

Fakebooks or **Chord Books** are books that contain **Lyrics and Chords**.

Instead of transcribing chords on your own, you can just buy ready made fakebooks as save yourself some time. And unlike getting the chords and lyrics online, getting a fakebook assures you that the chords and lyrics would be **100% accurate**.

Here are my **Top 5 Fakebooks**:

*   The Easy Fakebook - webspicer.com/piano/fakebook1
*   The Ulimate Fakebook - webspicer.com/piano/fakebook2
*   The Ultimate Pop Rock Fakebook - webspicer.com/piano/fakebook3
*   The Classic Rock Fakebook - webspicer.com/piano/fakebook4
*   The Ultimate Country Fakebook - webspicer.com/piano/fakebook5

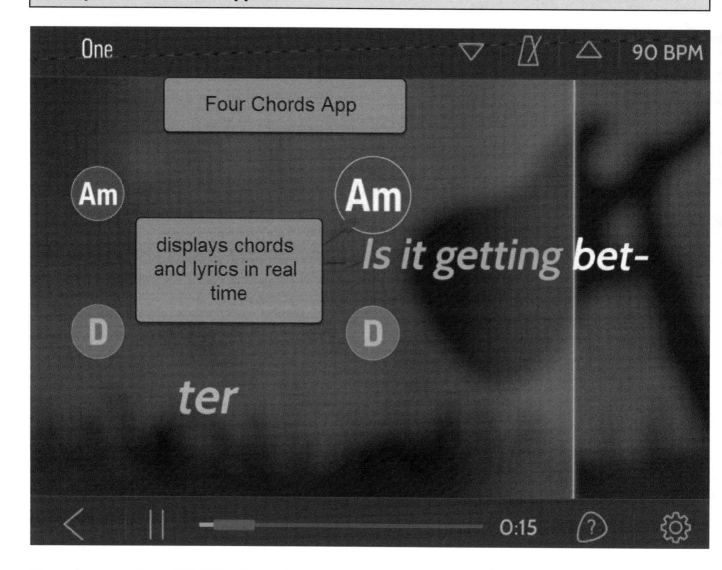

There are also a lot of **Mobile Apps** that you can use to **practice playing chords**. My favorite app so far is called **Four Chords**. I like it because it only displays songs that can be played using the **Chords in the Major Scale**.

Apps that play chords and Lyrics in real time:

* Four Chords - webspicer.com/piano/four-chords
* Riffstation - webspicer.com/piano/riffstation
* Jamn - webspicer.com/piano/jamn

Apps that find the chords and lyrics for you:

* Jellynote Guitar Chords - webspicer.com/piano/jellynote
* Achording - webspicer.com/piano/achording
* Ultimate Guitar - webspicer.com/piano/ultimate

Apps that you can use to save your own lyrics and chords:

• OnSong - webspicer.com/piano/onsong

Online Tools

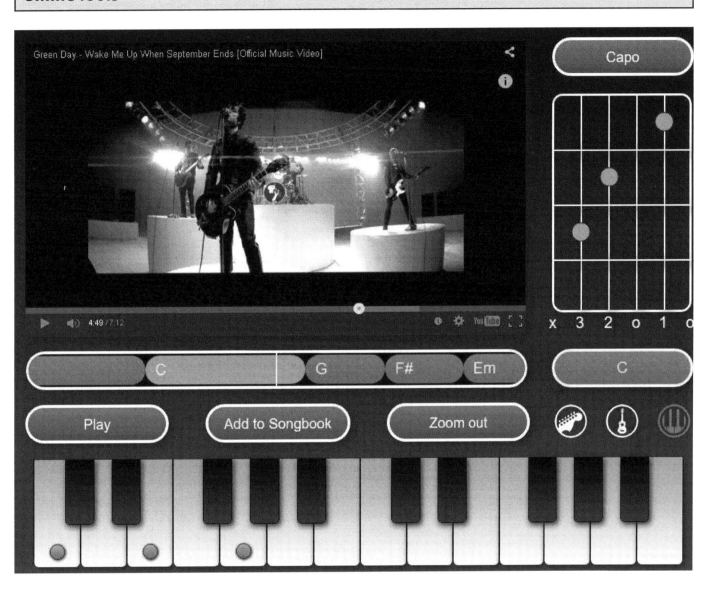

Here are a couple of cool online tools that will extract the chords for you. Just find the videos on Youtube and paste it in the web app.

Chordify - chordify.net
Riffstation Online - play.riffstation.com

Here's a website that let's you download **songs without piano** accompaniment.

bit.ly/karaoke-version

Riffstation is a software that automatically extracts the chords from an MP3 file. What's nice about this software is that you can transpose the song to any key, and even slow it down so you can learn how to play it.

You can download Riffstation here:

https://riffstation.com/

Final Words

Congratulations! You have just learned the secrets of playing the piano the easy way.

I hope that you enjoyed reading and learning from this book as much as I enjoyed writing it . I put a lot of effort to make the book easy to read and be very informative at the same time.

The most **important thing** you need to do now is to **take action**. Go to your piano and try the exercises that you found in this book. Information is useless if it is not applied.

Good luck and have fun playing the piano!

Paolo S. Ocampo
webspicer.com

Get in touch!
If you found this book helpful, please do leave me a **review** here:

bit.ly/piano-feedback

Your comments and feedback are greatly appreciated.